Simply, little poems

John O'Connell

Simply,
little poems

Simply, little poems
ISBN 978 1 76109 301 2
Copyright © text John O'Connell 2022
Cover drawings, sumi on cotton, by the author

First published 2022 by
GINNINDERRA PRESS
PO Box 3461 Port Adelaide SA 5015
www.ginninderrapress.com.au

Contents

Four Mile Beach	7
Newell Beach	24
New Guinea Highlands	25
The Daintree	26
Central Australia	30
Over Bourke and Longreach	31
Central India	32
Japan	39
Port Douglas	51
Letter to an unsigned bowl	56
Central Australia	59
The Snowy Mountains	63
Braidwood	77
North Queensland	78

the brilliant colours
have lightened at the horizon
and then, Surya appears, his chariot
and his seven white horses
bringing a new day

Four Mile Beach

early morning
clouds are drifting
to the west the moon
lighting the beach, casting
palm tree shadows

5 a.m. moonlight
the deserted beach

hushed sound
the ebbing tide

distant flash
the Low Isle light

here
in the stillness
of the sea, its reflection
the morning star high
in the eastern sky

the silence
has a certain sound
about it, the early birds
provide the clue, the sky
confirms it's morning

on the beach
and ebbing tide
the morning sky
is being painted
in watercolour

there is fire
on the horizon
clouds are burning
brilliant reds and yellow
orange, and then, the sun appears

yesterday's castles
have been washed away
all the footprints and the
lovehearts, everything
erased by the tide

the pelican
from the south, gliding
over the sea, lowers its skid-feet
for a perfect landing
and settles

this morning
the two dolphins
arching gracefully
through the sea
heading south

the summer
sea is rushing, stretching
across the dry-sand beach, to reach
the high tide mark
on time

the day
has been coloured in
clear blue for the sky, blue-green
for the sea, bright sunlight
dancing there

a scud, a squallish day
wind from the south-east
and the heavy black clouds
signalling the build-up
to the wet season

then, in the stillness
in the afternoon
the rain came
bringing music
and quiet colours

in watercolour
in a few brushstrokes
much practised, the painter
painting impressions
of the sea

in the sparkle
of afternoon light
unexpectedly, Ulysses
in stunning blue
drifts past

it is one of the pleasures
of holiday time, hearing
from a summer-filled
garden the laughter
of children playing

curlews call
across the silence
waves break a soothing
continuo while evening
settles down to night

Newell Beach

hot summer sun-
light reflecting
on the wrinkles
the cooling breeze
coming in from the sea

New Guinea Highlands

the morning sunlit cloud
rising from the valley again
inclosing the afternoon
in peacefulness
and rain

The Daintree

cloud
is stretching
just resting there
on the mountain
beautifully

as the ferry
makes its crossing
you can feel cool air
a breeze coming
up the river

I am contemplating the damp red earth
leaf-littered, there are sounds of a
stream and of birds, there are
tall trees buttressed, the
greens, browns, the
forest is filled
with light

morning has reached
a rainforest river
where fish swim
against the flow
dragonflies hovering

Central Australia

desert colours
browns and greens
dissolving into blues
of distant ranges
and the sky

Over Bourke and Longreach

from 34,000 feet
the patterns and light
colours of momentary
landscapes painted
so exquisitely

Central India

outside his mud-brick house
a potter is squatting
turning his wheel
forming a bowl
cutting the bowl
from the mound of clay
forming another small tea bowl

chai garam, chai garam
the tea sellers call
from the platform

passengers leave
others board the train
moves on slowly into the night

on the crowded third-class train
travelling slowly into the night
they brought much pleasure
the unglazed clay bowl
perfect for holding
and delightful
hot tea

the small
soft-fired bowl
crushed in the hand
is like a beautiful flower
withering and falling down
to the ground, its purpose
having been fulfilled

we can explain
how the bowl is made

but how do we explain
its mysterious beauty?

we persevere
making making making

we look
for thousands of years

and then
the answer comes

it is like a koan
a question of insight

Swami lit the oil lamp

this will be our light, he said
until the sun returns

Japan

Buddhist monks
returning from China
brought young tea bushes
which we call *Camellia sinensis*
for the leaves for the tea
to help them stay alert
whilst meditating

and they practised
chado, the way
of tea, the way
of modesty, humility
of simplicity and respect

a long time ago
the capital moved north
from Nara to Kyoto

in 1160, a teahouse was built
at Uji Bridge, a stopping place
for travellers along the road
between the old capital
and the new

over time
things have changed
a new bridge, a new teahouse
and still the original family
many generations on

in hills, near
the town of Uji
there are tea farms
set into fertile ravines
perfect for growing tea

having persevered for 15 years
to produce, in 1738, his prototype
green tea, the steaming and drying
fresh-picked leaves, he encouraged
others to use the process, so that
everyone might enjoy green tea
and his name? Sohen Nagatani

the house
where he was born
is still there, earthen
floor, thatched roof, shoji
screens, and serenely modest

in the silence
and soft filtered light
there are pickers picking
and the fragrance
of tea bushes

grown and
with much care
shaded at harvest time
steamed and dried, tencha
is stone-ground to make matcha

two chashaku, or scoops, that is
two grams of the matcha
hot water, not boiling
mindfully whisked
soft mellow tea

it is all in the care taken
in the preparation and the time
and the relaxation and contemplation
in conversation and in the serving
and the pleasure of sharing
in the experience
of tea

Port Douglas

the garden
is filled with sunlight
and colour, there is a sea breeze
and the sparkling music
of a fountain

slow wheel
quietly turning turning
the potter, making chawan, listening
and the clay speaking
silently

chawan, tea bowls
are quite wide and deep
and held in a particular way
with the left hand underneath
the right hand on the side

a simple, well-mannered bowl
is a most wonderful form
warm in the hands
and a pleasure
to be with

chawan
well cared-for
used and enjoyed
have dignity, they grow old
gracefully, they have a beautiful patina

Letter to an unsigned bowl

dear bowl,
you are destined
to grow old being
used and loved,
never famous
or precious,
but loved

oh, the wonder
of what is happening
in there, in all that heat
in the silence, glaze melting
and the bowls are coming to life

a bowl
with a flaw
a favourite bowl

despite the flaw, or
perhaps, because of it
true beauty is revealed

Central Australia

I'm remembering
being out on the Barkly
being woken by the sounds
of the cattle, waiting
for the sunrise

day after day
the small trees cast
shadows, resting places

it rains

and the vast dry plain
turns to green

the outback
sun-dried grass
the miraged horizon
is like a tree-lined lake
just waiting to be named

with the rain
the earth shines
desert flowers come
there is the freshness
it is like a new beginning

The Snowy Mountains

always, the wonder
the same overwhelming
sensation, the recognition
the sublime remembering
the being home again

oh, to find those elusive words
the words to describe the indescribable
the exquisite, the intangible
the fragile beauty
of landscape

the peacefulness
of the rain falling
almost imperceptibly
and the quiet greyness
of an early summer morning

a snow-melted
mountain stream
is making its music
beautifully cascading
over worn-smooth granite

winter snow
has melted
into streams
revealing granite
and where flowers grow

and now
summer grasses
and the flowers
return, redrawn
in soft pencil colours

above Whites River
there is soft snow grass
where cattle used to come
to summer over, grazing
on the Rolling Ground

at the edge
of the trees, a hut
sitting silently, watching
storms come and go
and the snow

Bogong Creek
comes tumbling
noisily over rocks
on its way to meet
the Crackenback

the track climbs
crossing a snow-grass
meadow where billy buttons
daisies and buttercups grow and up
through the snow gums and the granite
to about 1800 metres, there emerging
onto a pristine alpine landscape

in the silence
from rocky peaks
crows call, calling
a lone pilgrim
to prayer

there, in every
sound and nuance
an old man is taking
in his homeland, knowing
he might never come here again

cloud is passing
over the mountain creating

an idle interlude

sunshine defines the mountain
is coming back to life

today
the moon and the stars are resting

tonight
they will guide us home

Braidwood

clouds so heavy
that the cold wind
can barely move them

the lingering warm grey smoke
from kitchen fires, suddenly
blown away by the wind

North Queensland

in August
above the sea
on leafless trees
displays of yellow
kapok flowers

the yellows
of bananas and
the mangoes, the reds
of dragon fruit, grown there
and sold there, at the farm store

it just turned up
in the garden, a weed
a nuisance, then, one day
there amongst the prickles
a delicate flower appeared

they came
as beautiful gifts
simple, everyday things
not precious, but appreciated
and to be celebrated, in little poems

like the sun
in winter, a beautiful smile
has filled the day

www.ingramcontent.com/pod-product-compliance
Lightning Source LLC
Chambersburg PA
CBHW062146100526
44589CB00014B/1706